MRS. PELOKI'S SNAKE

Story by Joanne Oppenheim

Pictures by Joyce Audy dos Santos

DODD, MEAD & COMPANY   New York

Text copyright © 1980 by Joanne Oppenheim
Illustrations © 1980 by Joyce Audy dos Santos
All rights reserved
No part of this book may be reproduced in any form
without permission in writing from the publisher
Printed in the United States of America

1 2 3 4 5 6 7 8 9 10

Library of Congress Cataloging in Publication Data

Oppenheim, Joanne.
  Mrs. Peloki's snake.

  SUMMARY: The report of a snake in the boys'
bathroom causes quite a stir in Mrs. Peloki's
classroom.
  [1. Snakes–Fiction. 2. School stories]
I. Dos Santos, Joyce Audy. II. Title.
PZ7.O616Mi   [E]   79-6632
ISBN 0-396-07810-9

This book is for my father, who always said we worry about the wrong things.

—J.O.

To my mother, Marie Audy.

—J.A.dS.

We were thinking up words that rhyme with "lake,"
and I was just about to say "cake," when Kevin came running
out of the bathroom yelling,

"Snake!"

"Kevin! I'm surprised at you," said Mrs. Peloki. "You took Stephanie's turn. Raise your hand if you have something to say."

"But Mrs. Peloki," Kevin's voice was shaking. "I'm trying to tell you. *Snake*. There's a snake in the boys' bathroom."

"A snake?" she said and laughed. "It's the middle of winter, Kevin. Snakes hibernate."

"Not this one," Kevin insisted. "I saw it."
"Oh, no!" screamed Angie.
"Let me see it," Billy yelled, running toward the bathroom.

"Sit down, Billy," said Mrs. Peloki. "Now, children, it can't be a snake." She smiled at Kevin. "Maybe what you saw was a worm."

"Did you ever see a worm this big?" Kevin asked.

"Oh, dear," said Mrs. Peloki. She wasn't smiling any more.

"Listen," James said in a scary voice, "do you hear something rattling?"

"I want to go home," cried MariEllen.

"Let me out of here!" screamed Wendy.

"Me, too!" yelled Danny. "I hate snakes. I hate 'em."

"Mrs. Peloki," I called, but she didn't hear me because Billy yelled, "I'll get the snake. I'll cut it in pieces," and ran for the door. And James started slithering on the floor, sticking his tongue in and out.

And then Wendy yelled, "Get away from me, James."

"Ouch," Eddie hollered. "Marlon's throwing spitballs, Mrs. Peloki."

"I didn't do nothing," said Marlon. He always says that.

Mrs. Peloki grabbed Billy. "Boys and girls, please! Enough. James, Marlon, be quiet."

"Mrs. Peloki!" I raised my hand.

But all she said was, "Not now, Stephie. I'm sure it's nothing, but I'm going in to have a look at this snake."

Mrs. Peloki was acting real brave—at least for Mrs. Peloki. Once I brought a toy snake for show-and-tell and she wouldn't even touch it.

"There's nothing to be scared of, nothing to worry about," she kept saying. "I just need to find a stick or something." She picked up the yardstick.

"You going to measure it?" asked Billy.

"Of course not—but—I can't just pick it up in my hands.

Now Kevin," she whispered, as if she was afraid the snake would hear her. "Where did you see it? Under the sink or near the door?"

"Huh-uh. Next to the toilet," Kevin replied.

"All right, you hold the door open." Kevin grabbed the handle.

"Not yet! I'll tell you when. Just remember, keep the door open. Understand?" Kevin nodded. Everyone was silent.

"Okay, Kevin. Open it."

Two seconds later Mrs. Peloki came running out of the bathroom.

She was yelling, "Close it! Close it, Kevin! I saw it! I saw the snake!"

"I want to go home," MariEllen bawled.
"I'm getting out of here!" shouted Danny.
"I got to go!" said Marlon.
"Danny! Marlon! Everybody sit down!"
"But I got to *go!*" said Marlon.

"Sit *down*."

"I got to go real *bad*, Mrs. Peloki. An emergency."

"Well, go in the girls' room, then."

"I'm not going to no girls' room," said Marlon.

"Please — Marlon, everybody, settle down."

Mrs. Peloki flashed the lights on and off, but it didn't do any good. "Angie," she called, "go down to the office.

Tell them to send someone. Hurry."
"Mrs. Peloki!" I tried to get her to listen, but Billy yelled,

"James. Watch out! Under your chair. It's there!"
"Where?"

"The snake!" MariEllen screamed, without even looking.

"He's lying," yelled Marlon.
"I'll get you, Billy!" James ran for Billy.
Mrs. Peloki got between them. "James! Billy! No fighting."
"I'm going home," MariEllen wailed. "I don't feel good."
Mrs. Peloki didn't know what to do. So, while she wasn't looking, I picked up the yardstick and...

sneaked into the bathroom. I was trying to tell her all along.
I'm not scared of snakes.

"Come out of there, Stephie! It'll bite you!" I heard Mrs. Peloki shout.

"Don't worry. It won't hurt me. I'll show you."

"I don't want to see it," Mrs. Peloki yelled. "Just come out!"

"Okey-dokey, Mrs. Peloki. Stand back. I've got it. I'm coming out."

I came out dangling it in the air. "Here's your snake!" I said. It was nothing but a fat gray string from a dirty old mop.

"That?" exclaimed Mrs. Peloki. "I don't believe my eyes."
"It looked like a snake to me. Honest." Kevin's ears turned all red.

"You call that a snake?" said Billy. "I'm bringing a real one tomorrow."

MariEllen was still too scared to look.

"Can I go now?" asked Marlon.

Mrs. Peloki laughed till tears rolled down her cheeks.

"What a snake! Such a silly mistake. It seemed so real."

"A mistake. A snake," I said to myself, and then I remembered something. "Listen, Mrs. Peloki. You just made a rhyme. A *snake* mis*take*. And I know another."

"Tell us," she said.

"That's a *FAKE SNAKE*."